ACO-3976

Levers

by Anne Welsbacher

Consultant:
Philip W. Hammer, Ph.D.
Assistant Manager of Education
American Institute of Physics

Bridgestone Books
an imprint of Capstone Press
Mankato, Minnesota

Bridgestone Books are published by Capstone Press
151 Good Counsel Drive, P.O. Box 669, Mankato, Minnesota 56002
http://www.capstone-press.com

Library of Congress Cataloging-in-Publication Data
Welsbacher, Anne, 1955–
    Levers/by Anne Welsbacher.
    p. cm.—(The Bridgestone Science Library)
    Includes bibliographical references and index.
    Summary: Uses everyday examples to describe levers as simple machines used to lift,
push, or move a load.
    ISBN 0-7368-0611-3
    1. Levers—Juvenile literature. [1. Levers.] I. Title. II. Series.
TJ182.W45 2001
621.8′11—dc21

00-025613

Editorial Credits
Rebecca Glaser, editor; Linda Clavel, cover designer; Kia Bielke, illustrator; Katy Kudela,
    photo researcher

Photo Credits
David F. Clobes, cover, 4, 10, 14, 20
Jack Glisson, 8, 18
Kimberly Danger, 12
Unicorn Stock Photos/Jim Shippee, 16

1 2 3 4 5 6 06 05 04 03 02 01

Table of Contents

Simple Machines

Simple machines make work easier or faster. Work is using force to move an object across a distance. Moving and lifting are kinds of work. A lever is a simple machine. People use levers to lift heavy objects that they cannot lift by themselves.

force
anything that changes the speed, direction, or motion of an object

5

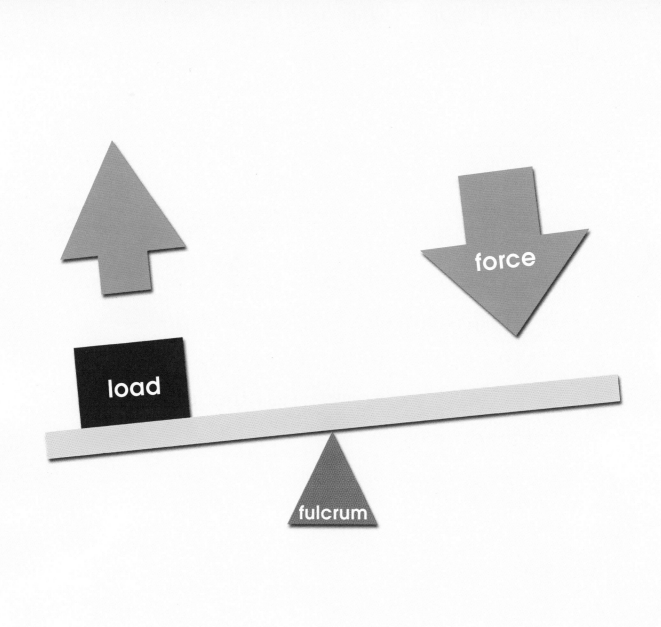

Parts of a Lever

A lever is a long, stiff bar. The bar rests on a point called the fulcrum. The fulcrum does not move. Force is put on one end of the lever. The other end lifts a load.

Using Levers

Levers move many kinds of loads. A bottle opener lifts a tight bottle cap. People use shovels to lift loads of dirt. A person uses oars to row a boat through water.

force

fulcrum

load

Near and Far

A lever's load, force, and fulcrum can be in different places. Moving a load placed near the fulcrum takes less force. A shovel is a lever. One hand is the fulcrum. Your other hand is the force. You can lift the load more easily if the fulcrum is closer to the load.

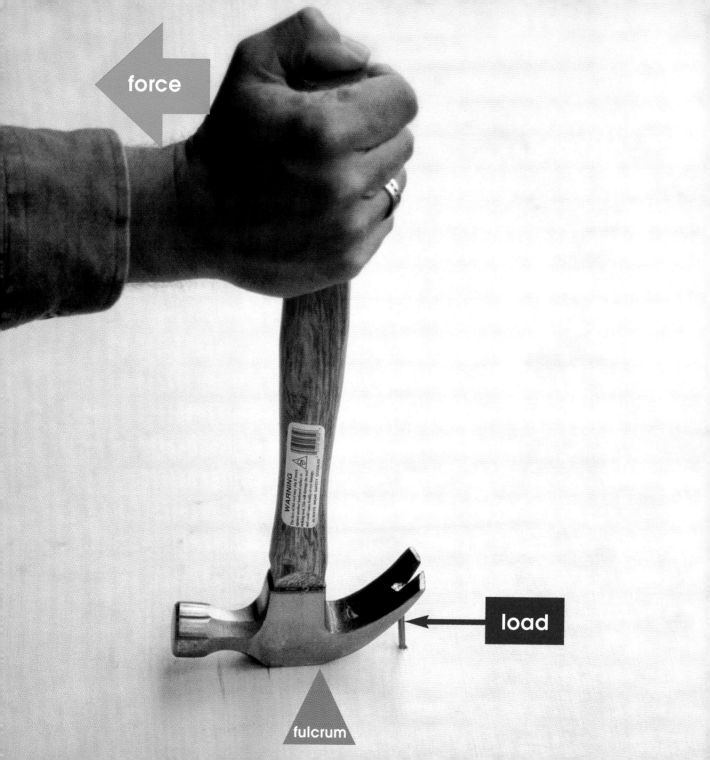

First-Class Levers

Some levers have the fulcrum between the force and the load. A person puts force on one end to move the load on the other end. These levers are first-class levers. A hammer pulling out a nail is a first-class lever.

Second-Class Levers

Second-class levers have the fulcrum at one end. The load is in the middle. Force is put on the other end. A wheelbarrow is a second-class lever. The load is close to the fulcrum of the wheelbarrow. A person can lift the load with less force.

Third-Class Levers

A third-class lever has the fulcrum on one end and the load at the other end. The force is in the middle. Third-class levers add reach. A hockey skater moves one end of the stick a short distance. The other end of the stick moves a longer distance to hit the puck.

Compound Levers

Levers can work together with other levers. A scissors is an example of a compound lever. Each half of a scissors is a first-class lever. They are joined at the fulcrum. Scissors cut paper more easily when the paper is close to the fulcrum.

compound
having two or more parts

Levers in Complex Machines

Simple machines often are part of complex machines. A piano uses many levers. Each piano key has a set of levers. The levers push a soft hammer. The soft hammer hits a string to make a sound.

complex
having many parts

Hands On: Near and Far

The fulcrum on a lever can be in many places. This activity will show you where to place the fulcrum to lift something using the least amount of force.

What You Need

Thin cardboard   Scissors
Masking tape   Wooden ruler
Small eraser   Large open area

What You Do

1. Cut a rectangle about 3 inches by 4 inches (8 centimeters by 10 centimeters) from the cardboard.
2. Fold the cardboard in three sections as shown at right. Put masking tape over the top to form a triangle. This cardboard triangle is the fulcrum.

3. Place the middle of the ruler on the fulcrum.
4. Place the eraser on the lower end of the ruler. The eraser is the load.
5. Press your hand down quickly on the other end of the ruler. Your hand is the force. How far did the eraser move?
6. Move the ruler so the fulcrum is farther from the middle.
7. Press your hand down quickly on the other end. How far did the eraser move?

Try placing the fulcrum and load in different places. What is the best combination for making the eraser fly the farthest? What combination uses the least force to lift the eraser into the air?

Words to Know

complex (kahm-PLEKS)—having many parts

compound (KOM-pound)—having two or more parts

force (FORSS)—anything that changes the speed, direction, or motion of an object

fulcrum (FUL-krum)—the point on which a lever rests

load (LOHD)—something that is moved

work (WURK)—using force to move an object across a distance

Read More

Armentrout, Patricia. *The Lever.* Simple Devices. Vero Beach, Fla.: Rourke, 1997.

Glover, David. *Levers.* Simple Machines. Crystal Lake, Ill.: Rigby Interactive Library, 1997.

Rush, Caroline. *Levers.* Simple Science. Austin, Texas: Raintree Steck-Vaughn, 1997.

Internet Sites

Inventors Toolbox: Simple Machines
http://www.mos.org/sln/Leonardo/InventorsToolbox.html
Levers
http://www.robinsonresearch.com/TECHNOL/the_lever.htm
School Zone, Simple Machines
http://www.science-tech.nmstc.ca/maindex.cfm?idx=1394&language=english&museum=sat&function=link&pidx=1394

Index